Somatic Yoga for Trauma Recovery and Healing

Healing the Body, Calming the Mind; Harness the Power of Mind-Body Connection to Overcome Past Pain and Find Inner Peace with Somatic Yoga Practices and Somatic Therapy.

Michelle W. Vogel

Copyright

Disclaimer

The exercises and advice contained within this book, "Somatic Yoga Exercises for Weight Loss," are intended for informational purposes only. They are not a substitute for professional medical advice, diagnosis, or treatment. The author, Michelle W. Vogel, and the publishers do not assume any liability for injuries or health conditions that may result from following the exercise routines presented herein.

Before beginning any new exercise program, including the somatic yoga exercises detailed in this book, it is recommended that you consult with your physician or healthcare provider. Individual weight loss results may vary, and the effectiveness of the exercises may differ based on individual fitness levels, body types, and commitment to the program.

The author and publishers have made every effort to ensure the accuracy and efficacy of the exercises and information presented, but they cannot guarantee that the techniques will be suitable for every individual reader. Readers are encouraged to approach the exercises with mindfulness and to adapt them to their personal capabilities and needs.

By using this book, you acknowledge and agree that you are doing so at your own risk, and you willingly accept responsibility for any potential adverse effects on your health.

Dedication

To all those who have faced the darkness of trauma and seek the light of healing. This book is dedicated to your courage, resilience, and unwavering spirit. May you find peace, strength, and renewal through the practice of Somatic Yoga. And to the loved ones who walk beside you, offering support and love, this journey is also yours.

TABLE OF CONTENTS

INTRODUCTION — 1

UNDERSTANDING TRAUMA AND ITS IMPACT — 2
THE POWER OF SOMATIC YOGA — 3
THE BODY-MIND CONNECTION — 4
PRACTICING SOMATIC YOGA FOR HEALING — 5
INTEGRATING SOMATIC YOGA INTO TRAUMA HEALING — 6
APPLYING SOMATIC YOGA IN EVERYDAY LIFE — 7
CONCLUSION AND APPENDIX — 7
YOUR JOURNEY TO HEALING — 8

OVERVIEW OF SOMATIC YOGA AND ITS BENEFITS FOR TRAUMA — 11

BENEFITS OF SOMATIC YOGA FOR TRAUMA — 12

EXPLANATION OF TRAUMA AND ITS EFFECTS ON THE BODY AND MIND — 15

THE PURPOSE OF THIS BOOK AND ITS STRUCTURE — 17

PART I: UNDERSTANDING TRAUMA AND SOMATIC YOGA — 19

CHAPTER 1: WHAT IS TRAUMA? — 21

DIFFERENT TYPES OF TRAUMAS — 22
HOW TRAUMA AFFECTS THE BODY AND MIND — 23

CHAPTER 2: INTRODUCTION TO SOMATIC YOGA — 27

EXPLANATION OF SOMATIC YOGA PRINCIPLES — 27
BENEFITS OF SOMATIC YOGA FOR TRAUMA HEALING — 30

CHAPTER 3: THE BODY-MIND CONNECTION IN TRAUMA   **33**

HOW TRAUMA IS STORED IN THE BODY   34
THE ROLE OF THE NERVOUS SYSTEM IN TRAUMA RESPONSES   36
HOW SOMATIC YOGA CAN HELP REGULATE THE NERVOUS SYSTEM   38

PART II: PRACTICING SOMATIC YOGA FOR TRAUMA HEALING   **43**

CHAPTER 4: PREPARING FOR SOMATIC YOGA PRACTICE   **45**

CREATING A SAFE SPACE FOR PRACTICE   45
UNDERSTANDING BODY SENSATIONS AND BOUNDARIES   48
BREATHING TECHNIQUES FOR RELAXATION AND GROUNDING   50
INCORPORATING BREATHING TECHNIQUES: 53

CHAPTER 5: BASIC SOMATIC YOGA PRACTICES   **55**

GENTLE MOVEMENTS TO RELEASE TENSION   55
BODY SCANS FOR AWARENESS AND RELAXATION   61

CHAPTER 6: ADVANCED SOMATIC YOGA PRACTICES   **65**

PROGRESSIVE MUSCLE RELAXATION   65
YOGA POSES FOR TRAUMA RELEASE AND GROUNDING   69
PARTNER OR GROUP SOMATIC PRACTICES FOR CONNECTION AND SUPPORT   75

PART III: INTEGRATING SOMATIC YOGA INTO TRAUMA HEALING   **79**

CHAPTER 7: SOMATIC YOGA FOR EMOTIONAL REGULATION   **81**

PRACTICES TO MANAGE ANXIETY AND PANIC ATTACKS   82
TECHNIQUES FOR PROCESSING AND RELEASING EMOTIONS SAFELY   88
USING SOMATIC YOGA AS A TOOL FOR SELF-SOOTHING   91
THE NEED FOR GUIDED IMAGERY IN SOMATIC YOGA FOR TRAUMA RECOVERY   99

CHAPTER 8: SOMATIC YOGA FOR POST-TRAUMATIC GROWTH   103

Cultivating Resilience through Somatic Yoga   103
Finding Meaning and Purpose in Trauma Recovery   106
Nurturing Self-Compassion and Self-Care Practices   110

PART IV: APPLYING SOMATIC YOGA IN EVERYDAY LIFE   115

CHAPTER 9: SOMATIC YOGA FOR DAILY STRESS MANAGEMENT   117

Incorporating Somatic Yoga into Daily Routines   124
Using Somatic Yoga to Enhance Overall Well-Being   126

RECAP OF KEY CONCEPTS IN THIS BOOK   129

Encouragement for Continued Practice and Self-Care   132
Appendix   133
Tips for Practicing Somatic Yoga with Specific Trauma Populations   138
Glossary of Somatic Yoga Terms   141

Introduction

Imagine standing at the edge of a vast, dark forest. The air is heavy, and the path ahead is shrouded in shadows, unknown and daunting. You know you have to move forward, but fear grips you. This is what living with trauma can feel like. Yet, just as the first rays of dawn pierce through the trees, offering light and hope, Somatic Yoga can guide you through the darkness, helping you find your way to healing and peace.

Welcome to "Somatic Yoga for Trauma Recovery and Healing," a comprehensive guide designed to empower you on your journey through the shadows of trauma into the light of recovery. This book is not just about yoga; it's about reclaiming your life, body, and mind from the clutches of trauma. Through the principles and practices of Somatic Yoga, you will learn how to reconnect with yourself, release stored pain, and build a sense of inner peace and resilience.

Understanding Trauma and Its Impact

Trauma can take many forms. It could be the result of a single catastrophic event, such as an accident or natural disaster, or it could stem from prolonged exposure to stress, such as in cases of abuse or combat. Trauma leaves deep imprints on the mind and body, affecting how you perceive and interact with the world around you. It disrupts your nervous system, leading to symptoms like anxiety, depression, hyperarousal, and emotional numbness.

The first part of this book, "Understanding Trauma and Somatic Yoga," explains the nature of trauma. We will look at its various types—acute, chronic, and complex—and how each uniquely impacts the body and mind. By understanding the mechanisms of trauma, you will gain insight into why you feel the way you do and how Somatic Yoga can help you heal.

The Power of Somatic Yoga

Somatic Yoga is more than a physical exercise; it's a holistic approach that integrates the mind, body, and spirit. Unlike traditional yoga, which often focuses on achieving perfect poses, Somatic Yoga emphasizes the internal experience of movement. It's about tuning into your body, noticing sensations, and allowing yourself to move in ways that feel nurturing and healing.

In "Introduction to Somatic Yoga," you will learn about the principles that underpin this practice. We will explore how Somatic Yoga differs from traditional yoga and why it is particularly effective for trauma recovery. This chapter sets the stage for understanding how gentle movements, breath awareness, and mindfulness can create profound shifts in your physical and emotional state.

The Body-Mind Connection

One of the core tenets of Somatic Yoga is the body-mind connection. Trauma is not just stored in the mind but also in the body. Your nervous system plays a crucial role in this process. When you experience trauma, your body goes into survival mode—fight, flight, or freeze. These responses, while necessary for immediate survival, can become ingrained, causing chronic stress and physical tension long after the danger has passed.

In "The Body-Mind Connection in Trauma," we will look at how trauma is stored in the body and the role of the nervous system in trauma responses. Understanding this connection is vital because it underscores why somatic practices are so effective. Somatic Yoga helps regulate the nervous system, promoting relaxation and grounding, which are essential for releasing trauma.

Practicing Somatic Yoga for Healing

Healing from trauma is a journey, and Somatic Yoga provides a gentle, supportive path. The second part of this book, "Practicing Somatic Yoga for Trauma Healing," offers a range of practices designed to help you release tension, increase body awareness, and promote relaxation.

"Preparing for Somatic Yoga Practice" guides you in creating a safe space for your practice, understanding your body sensations and boundaries, and using breathing techniques for relaxation and grounding. These preparatory steps are crucial for setting the stage for effective healing.

"Basic Somatic Yoga Practices" includes mild movements that relieve tension, body scans that promote awareness and relaxation, and mindful breathing exercises that soothe the nervous system. These foundational practices are accessible to everyone and can be done at your own pace.

For those looking to take their practice farther, the "Advanced Somatic Yoga Practices" introduces techniques like progressive muscle relaxation, specific yoga poses for trauma release and grounding, and partner or group activities that enhance connection and support. These advanced practices provide powerful tools for deeper healing and connection.

Integrating Somatic Yoga into Trauma Healing

The third part of the book, "Integrating Somatic Yoga into Trauma Healing," focuses on using Somatic Yoga to manage emotional regulation and promote post-traumatic growth.

In "Somatic Yoga for Emotional Regulation," you will find practices to manage anxiety and panic attacks, techniques for processing and releasing emotions safely, and ways to use Somatic Yoga as a tool for self-soothing.

Emotional regulation is a critical aspect of trauma recovery, and these practices offer practical, effective strategies to help you ease intense emotions.

"Somatic Yoga for Post-Traumatic Growth" explores how to cultivate resilience through Somatic Yoga, find meaning and purpose in trauma recovery, and nurture self-compassion and self-care practices. This chapter is about transforming your trauma into a source of strength and growth, using Somatic Yoga as a catalyst for positive change.

Applying Somatic Yoga in Everyday Life

The final part of the book, "Applying Somatic Yoga in Everyday Life," helps you integrate these practices into your daily routine. In "Somatic Yoga for Daily Stress Management," you will learn quick Somatic Yoga practices for busy days, how to incorporate Somatic Yoga into your daily routines, and how to use Somatic Yoga to enhance overall well-being. These practical tips and techniques make it easy to maintain a consistent practice, no matter how hectic your life may be.

Conclusion and Appendix

As we conclude this journey together, the "Conclusion" section will recap the key concepts of Somatic Yoga for trauma healing. It will offer encouragement for continued practice and self-care, reminding you that healing is a lifelong journey. You will also find resources for further reading and support, including recommended books, websites, and professional help.

The "Appendix" provides additional resources, such as Somatic Yoga sequences for specific trauma symptoms like insomnia and hyperarousal, tips for practicing Somatic Yoga with specific trauma populations (e.g., veterans, survivors of abuse), and a glossary of Somatic Yoga terms. These resources are designed to support you in your practice and provide guidance tailored to your unique needs.

Your Journey to Healing

Embarking on the path of Somatic Yoga for trauma recovery is an act of courage and self-love. This book is your companion on that journey, offering knowledge, tools, and support to help you heal and thrive. Each chapter is thoughtfully written with care, providing you with practical, accessible practices that you can incorporate into your daily life.

Remember, healing from trauma is not a destination but a journey. It requires patience, compassion, and dedication. By engaging with the practices in this book, you are taking a significant step towards reclaiming your life and finding peace.

Whether you are new to yoga or have years of experience, Somatic Yoga offers a gentle, effective way to connect with your body, release stored pain, and builds a sense of inner peace and resilience.

As you move forward, know that you are not alone. Countless others have walked this path before you, finding hope and healing through Somatic Yoga. You, too, can find your way through the shadows of trauma into the light of recovery. This book is here to guide and support you every step of the way. Embrace the journey, and may you find the peace and healing you deserve.

Overview of Somatic Yoga and its Benefits for Trauma

Somatic Yoga is a therapeutic practice that combines the principles of somatic movement and yoga to create a holistic approach to healing and well-being. The term "somatic" comes from the Greek word "soma," which means "body," and it emphasizes the mind-body connection and the internal perception of bodily sensations. Unlike traditional yoga, which often focuses on external postures and alignment, Somatic Yoga essential focus is on internal awareness, slow and mindful movements, and the release of tension stored in the body. It's emphasis is on the importance of somatic awareness and mindful movement in promoting healing and well-being.

Somatic Yoga helps in recognizing that trauma is not only stored in the mind but also deeply embedded within the body. Traumatic experiences can leave lasting imprints on our physical selves, manifesting as tension, pain, and discomfort. Moreover, trauma disrupts the natural flow of energy within the body, resulting in dysregulation of the nervous system and heightened states of arousal or dissociation.

However, through gentle, mindful movements and breath awareness, Somatic Yoga can gradually unravel the somatic residue of trauma, allowing individuals to release tension, restore balance, and reclaim a sense of safety and freedom within the body. Unlike traditional yoga which focuses primarily on external alignment and performance, Somatic Yoga invites you to cultivate an internal environment of sensation and awareness within, building a stronger connection with oneself and the present moment.

Benefits of Somatic Yoga for Trauma

- **Release of Stored Tension and Trauma:** Trauma often manifests in the body as chronic tension and pain. Somatic Yoga helps to release this stored tension through gentle, mindful movements. By addressing the physical manifestations of trauma, you can begin to heal both physically and emotionally.

- **Regulation of the Nervous System:** Trauma can dysregulate the nervous system, leading to symptoms such as anxiety, hypervigilance, and dissociation. The slow, mindful movements and breathwork in Somatic

Yoga help to calm the nervous system, promoting a state of relaxation and balance.

- **Enhanced Body Awareness:** Trauma can lead to a disconnection from the body, as individuals may numb or ignore bodily sensations to cope with distress. With Somatic Yoga, you can reconnect with your body, enhancing body awareness and helping you feel more present and grounded.

- **Reduction of Stress and Anxiety:** The mindfulness and relaxation techniques used in Somatic Yoga can significantly reduce stress and anxiety levels. This is particularly beneficial for trauma survivors, who often experience heightened stress responses.

- **Empowerment and Control:** Trauma can leave individuals feeling powerless and out of control. Somatic Yoga empowers you by giving you tools that will help you manage your own healing process. The practice encourages a sense of agency and control over one's body and responses.

- **Improved Emotional Regulation:** Somatic Yoga improves emotional understanding and regulation by creating a stronger connection between the mind and body. Improved emotional regulation can result in more stable and balanced emotional states.

- **Support for Trauma Processing:** Somatic Yoga provides a safe space for individuals to process and release trauma. The practice encourages a gentle exploration of traumatic experiences, allowing for healing and integration.

- **Holistic Healing:** Finally, it addresses the mind, body, and spirit, offering a holistic approach to trauma recovery. This comprehensive approach can lead to deeper and more lasting healing.

Explanation of trauma and its effects on the body and mind

Before we begin with our practice of Somatic Yoga, it's essential to understand the nature of trauma and its profound impact on the body and mind. Trauma is not just an event that occurs to an individual, but rather, a deeply distressing experience that overwhelms an individual's capacity to cope, leaving lasting imprints on their psyche and physiology.

Traumatic experiences can range from acute incidents, such as accidents or assaults, to chronic forms of adversity, such as prolonged abuse or neglect. Regardless of the specific nature of the trauma, its effects reverberate throughout the entire being, disrupting one's sense of safety, trust, and self-worth.

On a physiological level, trauma triggers a cascade of neurobiological responses within the body, activating the sympathetic nervous system's "fight-flight-freeze" response. This primal survival mechanism prepares the body to either confront or flee from perceived threats, flooding it with stress hormones like cortisol and adrenaline.

In cases of chronic or repeated trauma, the body may become stuck in a state of hyperarousal, leading to heightened vigilance, hypervigilance, and chronic stress. Conversely, some individuals may dissociate or shut down in response to overwhelming trauma, numbing themselves from their bodily sensations and emotions as a means of self-preservation.

The effects of trauma are not limited to the physical realm but extend deeply into the realm of the psyche and soul. Trauma can shatter one's sense of identity, disrupt their relationships, and undermine their fundamental beliefs about the world and themselves. Moreover, unresolved trauma can contribute to the development of various mental health disorders, such as post-traumatic stress disorder (PTSD), depression, and anxiety.

In the face of such profound adversity, the journey of healing from trauma requires a comprehensive and compassionate approach that addresses the multidimensional nature of human experience. Somatic Yoga offers a pathway towards healing that honors the interconnectedness of the body, mind, and spirit, inviting individuals to embark on a journey of self-discovery, resilience, and transformation.

The Purpose of this book and its structure

This book serves as a guide or tool for individuals seeking to harness the transformative power of Somatic Yoga in their journey of trauma recovery and healing. Drawing upon the principles of Somatic Yoga, mindfulness, and trauma-informed care, this book offers a comprehensive framework for cultivating somatic awareness, regulating the nervous system, and reclaiming a sense of wholeness and vitality.

The book has been structured into four parts, with part I serving as the laying blocks, or foundation for understanding trauma and the principles of Somatic Yoga. Part I explores the nature of trauma, the body-mind connection, and the unique benefits of Somatic Yoga for trauma healing.

In Part II, you'll be introduced to practical Somatic Yoga practices designed to promote relaxation, release of tension, and better embodiment. From gentle movements to mindful breathing exercises, these practices offer tangible tools for individuals to cultivate resilience and self-compassion.

Part III delves deeper into the integration of Somatic Yoga into the trauma healing process, offering specialized practices for emotional regulation, post-traumatic growth, and everyday stress management. By integrating Somatic Yoga into your daily life, you'll learn how to deal with the complexities of trauma with greater confidence, ease and resilience.

Finally, Part IV provides practical guidance on applying Somatic Yoga principles in various contexts, from self-care routines to therapeutic settings. Through accessible practices and insightful reflections, you can be empowered to embark on a journey of self-discovery and transformation, that will help you reclaim your innate capacity for healing and wholeness.

As we embark on this journey together, may this book serve as a beacon of hope and inspiration for all those who seek to transcend past pain and find inner peace through the transformative power of Somatic Yoga.

Part I: Understanding Trauma and Somatic Yoga

Understanding the relationship between trauma and the body is crucial for effective healing. Trauma is not just an event that happened in the past; it is an ongoing experience that can deeply affect a person's physical and mental well-being. Somatic Yoga offers a pathway to address these deep-seated effects by focusing on the body's sensations and movements, promoting healing from within.

In this part, we will explore the foundational concepts necessary to understand how trauma affects the body and mind, and how Somatic Yoga can facilitate recovery. This section will provide a comprehensive overview of trauma, detailing its various forms and how it manifests in the body.

We will also introduce the principles of Somatic Yoga and explain how it differs from traditional yoga practices. Finally, we will examine the body-mind connection in trauma and discuss how Somatic Yoga can help regulate the nervous system and support the healing process.

This part sets the stage for the practical applications and techniques discussed in the subsequent sections, equipping you with the knowledge needed to harness the power of Somatic Yoga in your trauma recovery journey.

Chapter 1: What is Trauma?

Trauma is a deeply distressing or disturbing experience that overwhelms an individual's ability to cope, causing feelings of helplessness and reducing their ability to feel a full range of emotions and experiences. Trauma can result from various incidents, ranging from a single event to prolonged exposure to adverse circumstances. The effects of trauma are not limited to psychological and emotional states but extend to physical health and well-being as well.

Trauma is often classified into different types based on its origin and duration. Understanding these types is crucial for recognizing how trauma affects individuals and for developing effective healing strategies.

Different Types of Traumas

1. Acute Trauma

Acute trauma results from a single distressing event, such as a natural disaster, car accident, physical assault, or sudden loss of a loved one. The event is typically unexpected and can leave the individual feeling shocked and overwhelmed. The immediate effects of acute trauma can include intense emotional reactions, such as fear, anxiety, and confusion. For instance, someone who survives a car accident may experience acute trauma, leading to symptoms like flashbacks, nightmares, and heightened anxiety when thinking about or encountering similar situations.

2. Chronic Trauma

Chronic trauma occurs from repeated and prolonged exposure to highly stressful events. This type of trauma often results from situations such as ongoing abuse (emotional, physical, or sexual), domestic violence, long-term illness, or living in a war zone. Chronic trauma can have pervasive and long-lasting effects on an individual's mental and physical health. For example, a child growing up in a household with an abusive parent may develop chronic trauma, which can lead to issues such as hypervigilance, emotional dysregulation, and difficulty forming healthy relationships.

3. Complex Trauma

Complex trauma is a result of exposure to multiple traumatic events, often of an invasive, interpersonal nature. These events are typically severe and pervasive, such as severe neglect, abuse, or exploitation, often occurring during critical developmental periods in childhood. Complex trauma can profoundly affect an individual's sense of self, their ability to regulate emotions, and their relationships with others. For instance, a person who has experienced repeated childhood abuse may struggle with feelings of worthlessness, trust issues, and difficulty maintaining stable relationships throughout their life.

How Trauma Affects the Body and Mind

Trauma has a several adverse effect on both the body and the mind, altering normal function and causing a variety of physical and psychological symptoms.

1. Physical Effects

Trauma is stored in the body, manifesting through various physical symptoms. The body's natural response to danger is to activate the fight-or-flight response, releasing stress hormones like adrenaline and cortisol. In the case of acute trauma, this response is temporary.

However, with chronic or complex trauma, the body remains in a heightened state of alert, leading to prolonged exposure to these stress hormones. This can result in physical symptoms such as headaches, muscle tension, chronic pain, fatigue, and digestive issues.

For example, a person who has experienced chronic trauma may develop tension headaches and muscle stiffness due to the continuous state of hyperarousal.

2. Psychological Effects

Trauma can lead to a range of psychological symptoms, including anxiety, depression, post-traumatic stress disorder (PTSD), and emotional numbness. These symptoms can impair an individual's ability to function in daily life and maintain healthy relationships.

For instance, someone with PTSD might experience flashbacks, intrusive thoughts, and severe anxiety, making it difficult to engage in normal activities or form meaningful connections with others.

Emotional numbness, a common response to trauma, can cause individuals to feel disconnected from their emotions and the world around them.

3. Cognitive Effects

Trauma can also impact cognitive functioning, affecting memory, attention, and decision-making abilities. Individuals who have experienced trauma may struggle with concentration, have difficulty remembering details of the traumatic event or other important information, and may experience confusion or disorientation.

For example, a trauma survivor might find it challenging to focus on work tasks or remember appointments, leading to frustration and decreased productivity.

4. Behavioral Effects

Trauma can influence behavior, leading to changes in how individuals interact with the world. This might include avoidance of certain places or activities that trigger memories of the trauma, increased irritability or aggression, substance abuse, and self-destructive behaviors.

A person who has experienced trauma might avoid social gatherings or places that remind them of the traumatic event, leading to social isolation and loneliness.

Understanding the multidimensional nature of trauma and its impact on the body and mind is critical to establishing successful healing and recovery solutions. Recognizing how trauma appears in numerous facets of life allows people to begin to treat its effects with practices such as Somatic Yoga, which promotes healing by linking the mind and body and instilling a sense of safety and well-being.

Chapter 2: Introduction to Somatic Yoga

Explanation of Somatic Yoga Principles

Somatic Yoga is an integrative practice that combines the principles of Somatic with traditional yoga. It emphasizes the internal experience of movement and the sensory feedback from the body, rather than focusing solely on achieving external postures or alignment. The core principles of Somatic Yoga include awareness, mindfulness, and the use of slow, deliberate movements to release tension and promote healing.

At the heart of Somatic Yoga is the concept of interoception, which is the awareness of internal bodily sensations. This practice encourages individuals to tune into their body's signals, fostering a deeper connection between the mind and body. By becoming more attuned to these sensations, you can identify areas of tension or discomfort and use gentle movements to release them.

Another key principle of Somatic Yoga is the emphasis on mindfulness and presence. You are encouraged to focus on the present moment, paying attention to your breath and bodily sensations without judgment. This mindful awareness helps to create a sense of safety and grounding, which is particularly beneficial for individuals recovering from trauma.

Somatic Yoga also incorporates the concept of neuroplasticity, the brain's ability to reorganize itself by forming new neural connections. Through repeated practice, Somatic Yoga helps to rewire the brain's response to stress and trauma, promoting a sense of calm and resilience.

How Somatic Yoga Differs from Traditional Yoga
While both Somatic Yoga and traditional yoga share common roots, they differ significantly in their approach and focus. Traditional yoga often emphasizes achieving specific postures (asanas) and alignment, with an external focus on how the body looks in each pose. In contrast, Somatic Yoga prioritizes the internal experience of movement and the body's sensory feedback.

In traditional yoga, the goal is often to perfect each pose and push the body to its limits. This can sometimes lead to a competitive mindset and a focus on external achievements. Somatic Yoga, on the other hand, encourages a non-competitive and self-compassionate approach. The emphasis is on gentle, slow movements that feel good to the body, rather than striving for perfection in poses.

Another key difference is the role of breath in each practice. While traditional yoga incorporates specific breathing techniques (pranayama) that are synchronized with movement, Somatic Yoga uses breath as a tool for mindfulness and relaxation. Practitioners are encouraged to breathe naturally and notice how their breath supports their movement and relaxation.

Somatic Yoga also places a greater emphasis on the nervous system and its role in trauma recovery. Traditional yoga practices can sometimes be too intense for individuals with trauma, potentially triggering a stress response. In contrast, Somatic Yoga's gentle approach helps to regulate the nervous system, making it a safer and more effective practice for trauma survivors.

Benefits of Somatic Yoga for Trauma Healing

Somatic Yoga offers numerous benefits for individuals recovering from trauma, addressing the physical, emotional, and psychological aspects of healing.

1. Physical Benefits

Somatic Yoga helps to release stored tension and trauma from the body through gentle movements and mindful awareness. This practice can alleviate physical symptoms such as chronic pain, muscle tension, and headaches. By improving interoception, you become more aware of your body's needs and can address areas of discomfort or tightness more effectively.

A trauma survivor experiencing chronic neck and shoulder tension can use Somatic Yoga to gently release these areas, reducing pain and improving overall physical well-being.

2. Emotional Benefits

Trauma can lead to intense emotional responses and difficulties in regulating emotions. Somatic Yoga helps to create a sense of safety and grounding, which is essential for emotional regulation. The practice encourages mindfulness and presence, allowing individuals to process and release emotions in a safe and supportive environment. By focusing on the body's sensations and the breath, practitioners can develop a greater sense of emotional stability and resilience.

> For instance, Somatic yoga can help someone with anxiety by calming their nervous system, which lowers panic attacks and promotes inner peace.

3. Psychological Benefits

Trauma often affects an individual's sense of self and their ability to engage with the world. Somatic Yoga promotes self-awareness and self-compassion, helping individuals rebuild a positive relationship with their bodies and themselves. The practice also supports neuroplasticity, enabling the brain to form new, healthier patterns of response to stress and trauma. This can lead to improved mental health, greater resilience, and a more positive outlook on life.

4. Holistic Benefits

Somatic Yoga's integrative approach addresses the interconnectedness of the body, mind, and spirit. By promoting a holistic sense of well-being, this practice supports overall health and vitality. The mindful movements and breath awareness foster a deep sense of relaxation and inner peace, enhancing the individual's quality of life.

Somatic Yoga offers a gentle, mindful approach to trauma recovery that honors the individual's unique experiences and promotes healing on all levels. This technique is an effective tool for overcoming previous pain and attaining inner peace because it promotes a stronger connection between the mind and body.

Chapter 3: The Body-Mind Connection in Trauma

Understanding and healing trauma requires a strong body-mind connection, and somatic yoga provides a powerful road to recovery. Trauma is more than simply a psychological event; it is deeply ingrained in the body, causing tension, discomfort, and dysregulation.

Somatic yoga, which emphasizes gentle movement, breathwork, and mindfulness, can assist to release these bodily manifestations of trauma. Individuals might begin to process and integrate traumatic events by paying attention to their bodily feelings and cultivating a compassionate awareness of the present moment.

This technique promotes a healthy interaction between the body and mind, allowing for the progressive discharge of accumulated trauma. Regular somatic yoga practice can help people develop more resilience, emotional regulation, and a renewed sense of safety and connection within their own bodies.

This comprehensive method not only relieves physical symptoms, but also promotes general healing and well-being, providing a revolutionary road to trauma recovery.

How Trauma is Stored in the Body

When a person experiences a traumatic event, the body's natural response is to enter a state of heightened alertness, also known as the fight-or-flight response. This response is designed to prepare the body to confront the threat or flee from it. However, if the traumatic event is overwhelming or prolonged, the body can remain in this state of heightened alertness for a long time, leading to the storage of trauma in the body.

One way trauma is stored in the body is through muscle tension. Muscles may contract in response to a distressing incident. If the trauma is not processed and released, the tension may become chronic, resulting in stiffness, pain, and other physical symptoms.

For example, a person who has been in a traumatic car accident may have persistent neck and shoulder strain as a result of their body's natural bracing during the impact.

Trauma can also be stored in the body via the neurological system. The autonomic nerve system (ANS), which regulates involuntary physiological activities, plays an important role in trauma responses. The ANS is made up of the sympathetic nervous system (SNS), which triggers the fight-or-flight response, and the parasympathetic nervous system (PNS), which promotes relaxation and healing. When a person is traumatized, the SNS becomes overactive, resulting in hyperarousal, whereas the PNS becomes underactive, hindering the body's capacity to recover to a state of calm.

Additionally, trauma can manifest in the body as somatic symptoms, such as headaches, digestive issues, and chronic pain. These symptoms can occur because the body's stress response can disrupt normal physiological processes. For instance, a person who has experienced ongoing emotional abuse might suffer from frequent stomachaches due to the constant state of anxiety and stress affecting their digestive system.

The Role of the Nervous System in Trauma Responses

The nervous system is central to the body's response to trauma. When a traumatic event occurs, the body's immediate reaction is mediated by the autonomic nervous system. The sympathetic nervous system (SNS) is activated, releasing stress hormones such as adrenaline and cortisol, which prepare the body for a fight-or-flight response. This activation results in increased heart rate, rapid breathing, heightened muscle tension, and a surge of energy. These physiological changes are designed to help the individual survive the immediate threat.

However, if the traumatic event is particularly overwhelming or prolonged, the body may remain in a state of heightened arousal even after the danger has passed. This prolonged activation of the SNS can lead to chronic stress, which has detrimental effects on both physical and mental health. Chronic stress can result in conditions such as hypertension, cardiovascular disease, anxiety disorders, and depression.

The parasympathetic nervous system (PNS) is responsible for

calming the body and promoting recovery after the threat has subsided. It slows the heart rate, reduces blood pressure, and promotes digestion and relaxation. In a healthy nervous system, the PNS effectively counterbalances the SNS, allowing the body to return to a state of calm after a stressful event. However, in individuals who have experienced trauma, the PNS may become less effective, leading to difficulties in regulating emotions and returning to a state of calm.

The nervous system's response to trauma can also include the freeze response, which occurs when fight or flight is not possible. This response is characterized by a state of immobility or dissociation, where the individual feels numb or disconnected from their surroundings. This can be a protective mechanism during extreme danger but can become problematic if it persists, leading to symptoms such as emotional numbness and dissociation.

How Somatic Yoga Can Help Regulate the Nervous System

Somatic Yoga is a potent technique for regulating the nervous system and supporting trauma rehabilitation. By focusing on the body's internal feelings and encouraging conscious movement, Somatic Yoga can promote overall health and well-being by restoring equilibrium between the sympathetic and parasympathetic nervous systems.

1. Promoting Interoception and Body Awareness

One of the key benefits of Somatic Yoga is its emphasis on interoception, the awareness of internal bodily sensations. Through practices such as body scans and mindful movement, individuals learn to tune into their body's signals and become more aware of areas of tension or discomfort. This heightened body awareness can help individuals recognize when their nervous system is in a state of hyperarousal or dissociation and take steps to bring it back into balance.

2. Encouraging Mindful Breathing

Breathing exercises are a central component of Somatic Yoga and play a crucial role in regulating the nervous system. Deep, mindful breathing activates the parasympathetic nervous system, promoting relaxation and reducing stress. Techniques such as diaphragmatic breathing and alternate nostril breathing can help calm the body and mind, making it easier to manage anxiety and other trauma-related symptoms.

Practicing deep belly breathing can signal to the nervous system that it is safe to relax, reducing the physiological effects of chronic stress.

3. Releasing Stored Tension

Somatic yoga uses slow, deliberate movements to help the muscles and fascia release tension that has built up. Individuals can safely explore tense areas and use movement to reduce tension by moving gently and attentively. This procedure helps to release the psychological and emotional components of trauma that have been stored in the body in addition to relieving physical symptoms like pain and stiffness in the muscles.

For instance, doing mild shoulder rolls and neck stretches will help relieve long-term stress in these regions, which can lessen headaches and increase general comfort.

4. Creating a Sense of Safety and Grounding

Trauma can disrupt an individual's sense of safety and grounding. Somatic Yoga practices such as grounding exercises and mindful movement help to reestablish a sense of connection with the body and the present moment. Techniques such as feeling the feet on the ground or engaging in slow, rhythmic movements can create a sense of stability and security, which is essential for trauma recovery.

Grounding poses, such as Mountain Pose (Tadasana), can help people feel more connected to the earth and their own bodies, creating a sense of safety.

5. Supporting Emotional Regulation

Somatic Yoga helps individuals develop tools for managing emotions and reducing the intensity of trauma-related responses. By practicing mindfulness and presence, you can learn to observe your emotions without becoming overwhelmed by them. Techniques such as progressive muscle relaxation (PMR) and gentle movement can help to calm the nervous system and promote emotional stability.

Practicing poses like the gentle forward fold can provide a calming effect, helping to reduce feelings of anxiety and promote a sense of inner peace.

6. Enhancing Neuroplasticity

Somatic Yoga supports the brain's ability to form new neural connections, a process known as neuroplasticity. By repeatedly practicing mindful movement and relaxation techniques, you can rewire your brain's response to stress and trauma, promoting resilience and well-being. This can lead to long-term improvements in mental health and emotional regulation.

For instance, regular practice of Somatic Yoga can help you develop healthier patterns of response to stress, reducing the likelihood of being triggered by reminders of past trauma.

In this session, we learned that Somatic Yoga offers a comprehensive approach to trauma rehabilitation by addressing the interdependence of the body and mind. Somatic Yoga promotes bodily awareness, attentive breathing, and the release of accumulated tension, thereby regulating the nervous system and supporting the healing process. This practice is a gentle and effective way to address the physical and emotional repercussions of trauma, promoting a sense of safety, grounding, and well-being.

Part II: Practicing Somatic Yoga for Trauma Healing

This section of the book focuses on the practical applications of Somatic Yoga for trauma therapy. While the preceding sections gave a theoretical understanding of trauma and the body-mind connection, This Part II focuses on practical methods and exercises that you can implement into your daily life to aid in trauma recovery. The goal is to provide a supportive and comfortable environment, increase awareness of bodily sensations, and learn effective techniques for releasing tension and regulating the nervous system.

Chapter 4: Preparing for Somatic Yoga Practice

Preparation is essential for a good Somatic Yoga practice, particularly for those struggling with trauma. This chapter walks you through the procedures necessary to create a secure and caring environment for your practice. It emphasizes the necessity of recognizing body sensations and respecting personal boundaries to ensure that the practice is comfortable and non-triggering. Furthermore, it provides basic breathing methods that encourage relaxation and grounding, laying the groundwork for deeper healing.

Creating a Safe Space for Practice

Creating a safe space for Somatic Yoga practice is essential, especially for individuals healing from trauma. A secure and supportive environment helps facilitate relaxation and encourages a deeper connection with the body, which is crucial for effective healing. Here are the key considerations for creating this space:

1. Physical Environment

Location: Choose a quiet and comfortable space where you can practice without interruptions. This could be a dedicated room, a corner of a room, or even an outdoor space, provided it's private and free from distractions.

Comfort: Ensure the space is comfortable. Use a yoga mat or a soft rug to practice on, and keep pillows and blankets nearby for added comfort and support during poses.

Ambiance: Create a soothing atmosphere by adjusting the lighting. Soft, natural light is ideal, but if you're practicing in the evening or in a darker space, consider using dimmable lights or candles. Scents can also enhance the ambiance; try using essential oils or incense with calming fragrances like lavender or chamomile.

Cleanliness: Keep the space clean and uncluttered. A tidy environment can reduce stress and help you focus more on your practice.

2. Emotional Environment

Privacy: Ensure your practice space is private, where you feel secure and won't be interrupted. This privacy is crucial for exploring and releasing emotions that may arise during practice.

Personal Touches: Add personal touches that make the space feel more like your own. This could include meaningful objects like photographs, plants, or artwork that inspire calm and positivity.

Boundaries: Establish clear boundaries with others in your household about your practice time. Inform them of your need for uninterrupted time to ensure you have the space to practice without concerns about disturbances.

Understanding Body Sensations and Boundaries

Understanding body sensations and establishing personal boundaries are fundamental aspects of preparing for Somatic Yoga practice. This knowledge will help you manage your practice safely and effectively, avoiding exacerbating trauma or discomfort.

1. Recognizing Body Sensations

Body Scanning: Begin with a body scan to become aware of the many feelings in your body. This technique entails mentally scanning your entire body from head to toe, noting any points of tension, discomfort, or relaxation. This increased awareness allows you to comprehend better how your body feels and identify areas that require attention.

Sensory Awareness: Pay attention to different sensory stimuli during your practice. Consider how your body feels on the mat, the texture of your clothing, and the sensations of your breath. Being attentive to these sensations can help you stay present and handle worry or intrusive thoughts.

Emotional Responses: Recognize that some sensations may elicit emotional responses. Allow yourself to express these feelings without judgment. Recognizing that these responses are normal will help you handle them more successfully.

2. Establishing Boundaries

Comfort Zones: Identify your physical and emotional comfort zones. Know your limits in terms of how far you can stretch or hold a pose. Avoid pushing yourself into discomfort, as this can lead to re-traumatization.

Consent with Yourself: Practice self-consent by checking in with yourself regularly. Before and during your practice, ask yourself if you feel comfortable and safe. If any pose or movement feels overwhelming, give yourself permission to modify or skip it.

Communication: If you're practicing with a partner or in a group, communicate your boundaries clearly. Let others know if you prefer not to be touched or if certain adjustments make you uncomfortable.

Breathing Techniques for Relaxation and Grounding

Breathing practices are central to Somatic Yoga, providing effective tools for relaxation and grounding. These strategies help to regulate the nervous system, relieve tension, and produce a sense of serenity and well-being. Below are some useful breathing strategies to include in your practice

1. Diaphragmatic Breathing (Belly Breathing)

Technique: Sit or lie down in a comfortable position. Place one hand on your chest and the other on your belly. Inhale deeply through your nose, allowing your diaphragm to expand and your belly to rise. Exhale slowly through your mouth, feeling your belly fall. The hand on your chest should remain relatively still.

Benefits: This technique promotes relaxation by activating the parasympathetic nervous system, reducing stress and anxiety.

2. 4-7-8 Breathing

Technique: Inhale quietly through your nose for a count of four. Hold your breath for a count of seven. Exhale completely through your mouth, making a whooshing sound, for a count of eight.

Repeat this cycle four times.

Benefits: This method calms the mind and body, reduces stress, and can help improve sleep quality.

3. Box Breathing (Square Breathing)

Technique: Inhale through your nose for a count of four. Hold your breath for a count of four. Exhale through your mouth for a count of four. Hold your breath for a count of four before beginning the next cycle. Visualize drawing a square with each breath phase.

Benefits: Box breathing helps focus the mind, enhance concentration, and manage stress.

4. Alternate Nostril Breathing (Nadi Shodhana):

Technique: Sit comfortably and use your right thumb to close your right nostril. Inhale deeply through your left nostril. Close your left nostril with your right ring finger and exhale through your right nostril. Inhale through your right nostril, then close it and exhale through your left nostril. Continue alternating for several cycles.

Benefits: This practice balances the nervous system, promotes mental clarity, and calms the mind.

5. Resonant Breathing (Coherent Breathing):

Technique: Inhale and exhale through your nose at a slow, steady pace, aiming for about five breaths per minute. Count to five on the inhale and to five on the exhale.

Benefits: Resonant breathing helps synchronize the heart rate and respiration, promoting a state of calm and relaxation.

Incorporating Breathing Techniques:

Begin and End Practices: Start and finish your Somatic Yoga sessions with a few minutes of focused breathing. This sets a calming tone for the practice and helps transition back to daily activities.

During Poses: Use breathing techniques to maintain relaxation and mindfulness during yoga poses. Breathe deeply and evenly to support your body and mind in each posture.

Daily Life: Practice these techniques outside of your yoga sessions to manage stress and anxiety in everyday situations. Integrate mindful breathing into your routine to enhance overall well-being.

Preparing for Somatic Yoga practice involves more than simply creating a physical space. It requires creating an atmosphere that promotes emotional safety, recognizing and honoring your body's sensations and limitations, and employing effective breathing techniques to promote relaxation and grounding. By addressing these issues, you can lay a solid foundation for your Somatic Yoga journey, increasing your ability to heal and grow through the practice.

Now that you are prepared; the next chapter will introduce you to basic Somatic yoga practices that are suitable for stress reduction and trauma recovery.

Chapter 5: Basic Somatic Yoga Practices

Building on the foundation of preparation, this chapter introduces you to basic Somatic Yoga practices for releasing tension, increasing body awareness, and promoting relaxation. Gentle movements are used to ease physical and emotional strain, while body scans help you connect with your internal experiences. Mindful breathing exercises are also covered, to show you how to harness the power of breath to calm the nervous system and cultivate a sense of inner peace.

Gentle Movements to Release Tension

Gentle movements are the foundation of Somatic Yoga, providing a gentle way to releasing physical and emotional strain. These exercises are intended to be slow and attentive, allowing you to focus on your body's sensations and responses. In this session, we will focus on some fundamental soft Somatic Yoga movement that will help you through your trauma recovery journey.

1. Cat-Cow Stretch

This is a gentle yoga flow that helps to improve spinal flexibility and release tension in the back and neck.

How to do this: Start on your hands and knees in a tabletop position. As you inhale, arch your back and lift your head and tailbone towards the ceiling (Cow Pose). As you exhale, round your spine and tuck your chin to your chest (Cat Pose). Move slowly and coordinate your breath with each movement.

Duration: 3–10 minutes

Repetitions: Aim for 3–8 repetitions

Benefits: The Cat-Cow stretch increases spinal flexibility, alleviates tension in the back and neck, and promotes a gentle massage for the internal organs.

2. Seated Forward Fold

How to do this: Sit with your legs extended straight in front of you. Inhale and lengthen your spine, then exhale and hinge at your hips to fold forward over your legs. Keep your spine long and your movements slow. You can place a cushion under your knees or use a strap around your feet for support.

Duration: 3–10 minutes

Repetitions: Aim for 3–5 times

Benefits: This gentle stretch releases tension in the hamstrings, lower back, and shoulders. It also calms the mind and relieves stress.

3. Shoulder Rolls

How to do this: Sit or stand comfortably with your arms relaxed by your sides. Inhale and lift your shoulders up towards your ears, then exhale and roll them back and down. Repeat this movement slowly and mindfully, paying attention to the sensations in your shoulders and neck.

Duration: 1–3 minutes

Repetitions: Repeat this gently movement for the stipulated time

Benefits: Shoulder rolls help release tension in the shoulders and neck, improve posture, and increase circulation in the upper body.

4. Pelvic Tilts

How to do this: Lie on your back with your knees bent and feet flat on the floor, hip-width apart. As you inhale, gently arch your lower back, creating a small space between your back and the floor. As you exhale, flatten your lower back against the floor by engaging your abdominal muscles. Move slowly and mindfully.

Duration: 3–8 minutes

Repetitions: 5–10 times

Benefits: Pelvic tilts release tension in the lower back and hips, strengthen the core muscles, and enhance awareness of the pelvic region.

5. Gentle Spinal Twist

How to do this: Sit with your legs extended in front of you. Bend your right knee and place your right foot on the outside of your left thigh. Inhale and lengthen your spine, then exhale and gently twist to the right, placing your left elbow on the outside of your right knee and your right hand behind you for support. Hold the twist for a few breaths, then switch sides.

Duration: Hold each twist for 30 seconds to 1 minute
Repetitions: 2–3 times

Benefits: Spinal twists release tension in the spine, improve digestion, and promote a sense of relaxation and balance.

Body Scans for Awareness and Relaxation

Body scans are a powerful technique for increasing body awareness and promoting relaxation. This practice involves mentally scanning different parts of your body, noticing any sensations without judgment. In this section, you will learn how to perform a complete body scan properly.

1. Preparation

First, you need to find a comfortable position, and then lie down on your back in a comfortable position. You can place a pillow under your head and knees for support. Close your eyes and take a few deep breaths to settle into your practice.

2. Scanning Process

The Feet: Begin by bringing your attention to your feet. Notice any sensations you feel, such as warmth, coolness, tingling, or tension. Simply observe these sensations without trying to change them.

The Body: Gradually move your attention up through your body, from your feet to your calves, knees, thighs, hips, lower back, abdomen, chest, shoulders, arms, hands, neck, and finally to your head. Spend a few moments focusing on each area, noticing any sensations that arise.

Stay Present: If your mind wanders, gently bring your focus back to the part of the body you were observing. The goal is to remain present and mindful throughout the scan.

3. Concluding the Scan

Once you have scanned each part of your body, bring your awareness to your entire body as a whole. Notice how you feel, and take a few moments to appreciate the sensations and relaxation you have created. Slowly begin to wiggle your fingers and toes, then gradually open your eyes. Take your time to transition back to your surroundings, moving mindfully and with awareness.

Benefits of Body Scans

Increased Body Awareness: Regular body scans help you become more attuned to your body's signals and sensations, enhancing your ability to respond to your needs.

Stress Reduction: By promoting relaxation and mindfulness, body scans can reduce stress and anxiety, creating a sense of calm and well-being.

Emotional Regulation: Understanding and acknowledging physical sensations can help you manage and process emotions more effectively.

Chapter 6: Advanced Somatic Yoga Practices

This chapter provides advanced Somatic Yoga techniques for people who want to take their practice to another level. Progressive muscle relaxation has been proven to be a means of gradually releasing tension throughout the body — and will be introduced in this chapter. The chapter also offers specific yoga positions that are especially good for trauma release and grounding, giving you tremendous tools to help in your healing process. It also highlights the benefits of partner or group somatic activities, which can help people feel more connected and supported during their recovery.

Progressive Muscle Relaxation

Progressive Muscle Relaxation (PMR) is a powerful technique for reducing physical tension and promoting overall relaxation. This method involves systematically tensing and then relaxing different muscle groups in the body. By doing this, you become more aware of the contrast between tension and relaxation, which helps to alleviate stress and anxiety.

1. Understanding PMR

The concept of PMR was developed by Dr. Edmund Jacobson in the 1920s as a way to help people manage stress and anxiety. The idea is to tense each muscle group firmly but not to the point of discomfort, and then to release the tension suddenly.

Benefits: This technique will help you to reduce physical tension and also improve your overall mental health by promoting a state of deep relaxation. It can also enhance your awareness of physical sensations and how your body responds to stress.

2. Practicing PMR

To perform PRM, you should start by finding a quiet, comfortable place where you won't be disturbed. Sit or lie down in a relaxed position, close your eyes, and take a few deep breaths to center yourself.

Sequence: The practice typically begins at the feet and progresses up through the body.

Simple, practical PMR sequence you can follow

Feet: Tense the muscles in your feet by curling your toes tightly. Hold for 5–10 seconds, then release and feel the relaxation spread through your feet.

Calves: Tighten your calf muscles by pointing your toes upwards. Hold for 5–10 seconds, then release.

Thighs: Squeeze your thigh muscles by pressing your legs together. Hold for 5–10 seconds, then release.

Abdomen: Tighten your abdominal muscles by pulling your belly button towards your spine. Hold for few seconds, then release.

Chest: Take a deep breath in, expanding your chest and holding the tension. Exhale and release.

Hands: Clench your fists tightly. Hold for 5–10 seconds, then release.

Arms: Tighten your biceps by bending your elbows and bringing your fists towards your shoulders. Hold for 5–10 seconds, then release.

Shoulders: Shrug your shoulders up towards your ears. Hold for 5-10 seconds, then release.

Neck: Gently press your head back into your pillow or chair. Hold for 5-10 seconds, then release.

Face: Scrunch up your facial muscles, including your forehead, eyes, and mouth. Hold for 5–10 seconds, then release.

Concluding the Practice: After completing the sequence, take a few moments to lie still and enjoy the feeling of relaxation. Notice any residual tension and consciously release it.

3. Tips for Effective PMR

Consistency: Practice PMR regularly to get the most benefit. Consistency helps you become more aware of your body's tension patterns and improves your ability to relax.

Mindfulness: Pay close attention to the sensations of tension and relaxation. This mindfulness enhances the effectiveness of the practice.

Gentle Approach: Avoid tensing muscles too forcefully. The goal is to create a contrast between tension and relaxation, not to strain your muscles.

Yoga Poses for Trauma Release and Grounding

Specific yoga poses can be particularly effective for releasing trauma and grounding the body. These poses are designed to help you connect with your body, release stored tension, and promote a sense of safety and stability.

1. Child's Pose (Balasana)

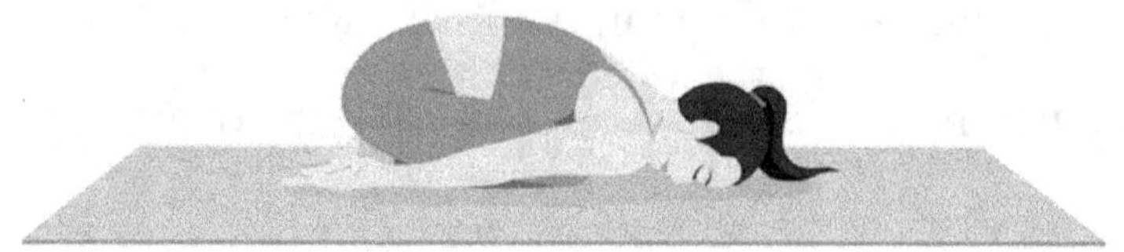

How to do this: Start on your hands and knees, then sit back on your heels and stretch your arms forward/backward, resting your forehead on the mat. Breathe deeply and relax your entire body.

Duration: stay in a pose for 30 seconds to 1 minute

Repetitions: 2–3 times

Benefits: The Child's Pose is a calming posture that helps release tension in the back, shoulders, and neck. It provides a sense of security and grounding, making it ideal for trauma recovery.

2. Legs Up the Wall (Viparita Karani)

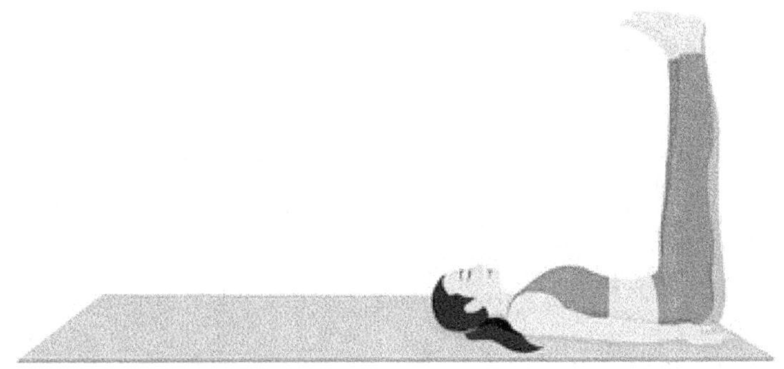

How to do this: Lie on your back with your legs extended up against a wall. Your hips can be close to or slightly away from the wall, depending on your comfort level. Relax your arms by your sides.

Duration: 1–3 minutes

Repetitions: 2–5 times

Benefits: This restorative pose promotes relaxation by enhancing circulation and reducing stress. It is particularly grounding and can help calm the nervous system.

3. Bridge Pose (Setu Bandhasana)

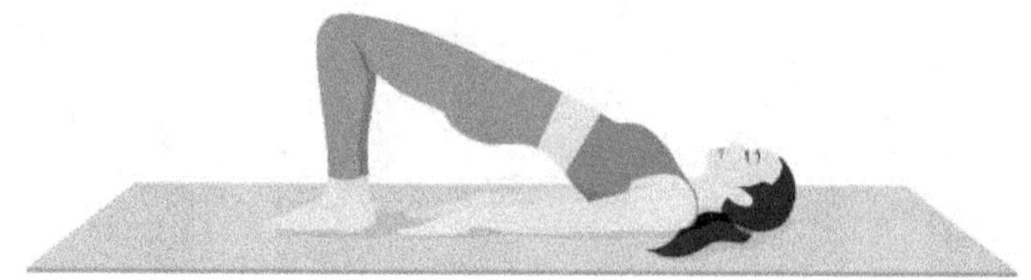

How to do this: Lie on your back with your knees bent and feet flat on the floor, hip-width apart. Press your feet into the floor and lift your hips towards the ceiling. Clasp your hands under your back and hold the pose for a few breaths.

Duration: 1–3 minutes
Repetitions: 2–5 times

Benefits: Bridge Pose opens the chest and strengthens the back muscles. It helps release tension in the spine and hips, promoting a sense of stability and grounding.

4. Reclined Bound Angle Pose (Supta Baddha Konasana)

How to do this: Lie on your back and bring the soles of your feet together, allowing your knees to fall open. You can place cushions or blocks under your knees for support. Rest your hands on your abdomen or by your sides.

Duration: 3–5 minutes

Repetitions: 1–3 times

Benefits: This gentle hip-opening pose releases tension in the hips and groin, promoting relaxation and emotional release. It also encourages a sense of openness and vulnerability in a safe way.

5. Corpse Pose (Savasana):

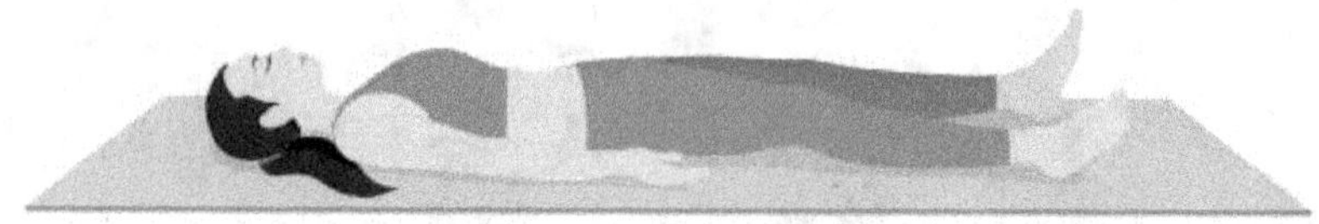

How to do this: Lie flat on your back with your legs extended and arms relaxed by your sides, palms facing up. Close your eyes and relax your entire body, focus on your breath, letting go of any tension or stress.

Duration: 10–15 minutes

Benefits: Savasana is the ultimate relaxation pose, it allows the body to fully integrate the benefits of the practice. It helps to ground the body, calm the mind, and release residual tension.

Partner or Group Somatic Practices for Connection and Support

Partner or group somatic practices can help the healing process by providing a sense of connection and support. These techniques entail interacting with others in a safe and supportive setting, which can be extremely beneficial to trauma rehabilitation.

1. Partner Breathing

How to do this: Sit back-to-back with a partner. Synchronize your breath so that you are inhaling and exhaling together. Feel the support of your partner's back as you breathe deeply and evenly.

Duration: 10–15 minutes

Benefits: Partner breathing helps build trust and connection. It promotes a sense of safety and mutual support, which is particularly beneficial for those recovering from trauma.

2. Mirroring Exercises

How to do this: Stand facing your partner. One person leads by performing slow, gentle movements, and the other mirrors these movements. After a few minutes, switch roles.

Duration: 10–20 minutes

Benefits: Mirroring exercises enhance empathy and connection. They help individuals become more attuned to each other's movements and emotional states, fostering a sense of understanding and support.

3. Group Circle Sharing

How to do this: Sit in a circle with a group of participants. Each person takes a turn sharing their experiences, thoughts, or feelings, while the others listen attentively without interrupting.

Benefits: Group circle sharing creates a safe space for individuals to express themselves and feel heard. It promotes a sense of community and support, which is vital for trauma recovery.

4. Supported Restorative Poses

How to do this: Practice restorative yoga poses with the support of a partner or group. For example, in Supported Child's Pose, one person can gently place their hands on the back of the person in the pose, providing a sense of grounding and support.

Duration: 5–10 minutes

Benefits: Supported restorative poses boost the advantages of the postures by adding an element of connection and reassurance. The physical presence of a partner or group member may improve the relaxation and encourage healing.

5. Group Guided Meditation

How to do this: Participate in a guided meditation session with a group. The meditation can focus on themes such as safety, grounding, and connection. The facilitator guides the group through the meditation, creating a shared experience of relaxation and mindfulness.

Benefits: Meditating with a guide in a group setting creates a powerful atmosphere of peace and connection. It lets you enjoy the well-known benefits of meditation while feeling the support and encouragement of those around you.

In summary, advanced Somatic Yoga practices, including progressive muscle relaxation, specific yoga poses for trauma release and grounding, and partner or group somatic activities, offer powerful tools for growing your practices and enhancing your healing journey. These techniques are designed to help you release physical and emotional tension and also promote a sense of connection, safety, and support, which are crucial for trauma recovery.

I believe this Part II has equipped you with the comprehensive toolkit of Somatic Yoga practices that address both the physical and emotional aspects of trauma. Through careful preparation, basic exercises, and advanced techniques, you should be fully guided towards a path of holistic healing, building resilience and a renewed sense of well-being.

Part III: Integrating Somatic Yoga into Trauma Healing

In this Part III, we'll dive deeper into incorporating Somatic Yoga practices specifically for trauma healing. This part goes beyond the foundational aspects covered in earlier sections and equips you with targeted techniques to address emotional regulation and post-traumatic growth.

This section emphasizes the practical application of Somatic Yoga as a tool for managing the emotional challenges associated with trauma. It guides you in utilizing poses, breath work, and mindful awareness to cultivate greater emotional stability, that brings about a sense of empowerment and control over your healing journey.

Chapter 7: Somatic Yoga for Emotional Regulation

Emotional regulation is a crucial aspect of trauma recovery. Trauma often disrupts the ability to manage emotions effectively, leading to heightened anxiety, panic attacks, and emotional dysregulation. This chapter explores how Somatic Yoga can help you regain control over your emotional responses, offering practical techniques to manage anxiety, safely process and release emotions, and use yoga as a self-soothing tool.

Our focus on this chapter, will be on Somatic Yoga practices specifically designed to help you manage and regulate your emotions. You will learn about practices that can reduce anxiety and panic attacks by grounding yourself and calming your nervous system. The chapter also covers techniques for processing and releasing emotions in a safe and controlled manner, ensuring that you can address emotional pain without becoming overwhelmed. Finally, you will discover how to use Somatic Yoga as a powerful tool for self-soothing, enabling you to comfort yourself during times of emotional distress.

Practices to manage anxiety and panic attacks

Anxiety and panic attacks can be overwhelming experiences, characterized by intense physical sensations like rapid heart rate, shortness of breath, and muscle tension. These attacks are common challenges for individuals recovering from trauma. Somatic Yoga provides several practices that can help manage these intense emotional states by grounding the body, calming the mind, and regulating the nervous system.

1. Diaphragmatic Breathing

This slow, deep breathing method triggers the parasympathetic nervous system, which is your body's relaxing response.

How to do this: Sit or lie down comfortably in a quiet space. Place one hand on your belly and the other on your chest. Inhale slowly through your nose, feeling your belly expand gently. Your chest should move minimally.
Exhale slowly through pursed lips, feeling your belly sink back down.

Practice for several minutes, focusing on the rise and fall of your belly with each breath.

2. Grounding Poses

Grounding poses are essential in connecting you to the present moment, helping you feel centered and secure. By focusing on your breath and the sensation of your body against the earth, these poses foster a deep sense of stability and calm. They allow you to release tension, reduce anxiety, and cultivate mindfulness, making them a powerful tool for emotional balance, trauma healing, and overall well-being. Engaging in grounding poses can also enhance your resilience to stress and trauma.

- ## **Mountain Pose (Tadasana)**

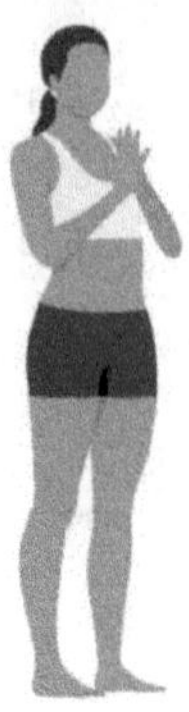

How to do this: Stand tall with your feet hip-width apart and press them firmly into the ground. Engage your core by gently drawing your belly button in towards your spine. Lengthen your spine and distribute your weight evenly through your feet. Close your eyes or soften your gaze if comfortable, and take a few deep breaths, feeling rooted to the earth.

Repetitions: Perform 5–10 repetitions during a yoga session.
Duration: Hold each repetition for 1–2 minutes.

Benefits: Grounding and centering the body promotes a sense of stability and tranquility. This grounding effect is very good for people suffering with anxiety and trauma recovery because it promotes a connection with the present moment and increases body awareness, lowering feelings of stress and confusion.

- ## **Butterfly Pose (Baddha Konasana)**

How to do this: Sit with your legs bent and the soles of your feet together. Hold your feet with your hands and gently press your knees toward the ground, allowing the hips to open. Keep your spine straight and focus on slow, deep breaths. This pose encourages relaxation and helps to open the hips, releasing stored tension.

Repetitions: Perform 3–5 repetitions during a yoga session.

Duration: Hold each repetition for 2–3 minutes.

Benefits: The Butterfly Pose stretches the inner thighs, hips, and groin, which can be areas of tension, especially in those dealing with anxiety or trauma. This pose promotes a sense of grounding and calm by focusing on breath and body awareness. It also aids in reducing stress by activating the parasympathetic nervous system, contributing to a sense of emotional release and mental clarity.

- ## **Side Body Stretch**

How to do this: Begin by sitting or standing with your spine straight. Extend one arm overhead and slowly lean to the opposite side, feeling the stretch along the side of your body. Keep your breath deep and even, focusing on the sensation of the stretch.

Repetitions: Perform 3–5 repetitions on each side

Duration: Hold each repetition for 1–2 minutes.

Benefits: The Side Body Stretch lengthens the muscles along the ribs, waist, and hips, enhancing flexibility and promoting deep breathing. It effectively relieves tension in the sides of the body caused by stress or anxiety and helps calm the nervous system.

- ## **Sphinx Pose**

How to do this: Lie on your stomach with your legs extended behind you. Place your elbows under your shoulders and gently lift your upper body, keeping your forearms flat on the ground. Allow your chest to open and breathe deeply, feeling the gentle stretch in your lower back and abdomen.

Repetitions: Perform 3–5 repetitions during a yoga session.
Duration: Hold each repetition for 2–3 minutes.

Benefits: The Sphinx Pose softly extends the spine and opens the chest, allowing you to breathe deeply and relax. It's fantastic for relieving lower back strain, which is typically exacerbated by stress or worry. This gentle backbend increases your body's relaxation response, which reduces anxiety and promotes tranquility.

3. Gentle Movement

Slow, mindful movements can help release pent-up tension and anxiety. Let's explore some gentle movements that are great for trauma recovery.

The Neck Rolls: Gently roll your head in a circular motion, five times forward and then five times backward.
Focus on the movement and breathe deeply throughout the rolls.

Shoulder Shrugs: Slowly shrug your shoulders upwards towards your ears, hold for a moment, and then release them down. Repeat this movement several times, focusing on releasing tension from your shoulders.

Techniques for Processing and Releasing Emotions Safely

1. Body Scans

Body scans promote awareness of physical sensations, allowing you to identify areas of tension related to anxiety.

- ## Full Body Scan

Lie down comfortably on your back and close your eyes.
Bring your attention to your toes and wiggle them gently.
Notice any sensations in your feet.

Slowly scan your body upwards, paying attention to any areas of tightness, pain, or discomfort.

Breathe deeply and allow yourself to simply observe these sensations without judgment.

Continue scanning your body all the way up to your head.

- ## Emotional Body Scan

Similar to the full body scan, but focus on areas where you feel emotional tension. Acknowledge the emotions present in each area, without judgment, and allow them to release through deep, mindful breathing.

2. Expressive Movement

• Shake It Out

Stand with your feet hip-width apart and shake your body vigorously for a few minutes, starting from your hands and moving to your feet. This movement helps release built-up emotional energy and tension.

• Dance Therapy

Put on some music and allow your body to move freely. Expressive dancing can help release emotions and improve mood by promoting the flow of energy through the body.

3. Sound Therapy

• Humming

Sit comfortably and hum softly, feeling the vibrations in your chest and throat. This simple practice helps release emotional tension and stimulates the vagus nerve, promoting relaxation.

• Chanting

Use mantras or simple sounds like "Om" to focus your mind and release emotional energy. Chanting can create a sense of calm and connection.

Using Somatic Yoga as a Tool for Self-Soothing

Self-soothing techniques are essential for managing stress and promoting emotional well-being, and Somatic Yoga offers a variety of practices that help calm the mind and body, building a sense of inner peace.

The Restorative Poses

The Restorative Yoga is a gentle practice focused on relaxation, reducing stress, and calming the mind. By incorporating restorative poses into your yoga practice, you can reduce stress, improve flexibility, and promote a sense of calm and well-being. Remember to always listen to your body and use props as needed to ensure comfort and support in each pose.

1. Supta Kapotasana (Reclining Pigeon Pose)

How to do this: Lie on your back with your legs extended. Bend your knees and place your feet flat on the floor. Cross your right ankle over your left thigh, just above the knee and then gently pull your left knee towards your chest, threading your right hand through the space between your legs to clasp your left thigh. Hold the pose and breathe deeply, feeling a stretch in your right hip.

Repetition: 1–3 times on each side.

Duration: 2–3 minutes on each side, allowing your body to relax.

Benefits: The reclining pigeon pose, promotes relaxation and stress relief by calming the nervous system, and also aid in the release of emotional stress stored in the hips, contributing to your overall well-being and emotional balance.

2. Supta Baddha Konasana (Reclining Bound Angle Pose)

How to do this: Lie on your back with your legs extended. Bring the soles of your feet together and allow your knees to drop out to the sides, forming a diamond shape with your legs. Place a bolster or pillows under your knees for support if needed. Rest your arms by your sides, palms facing up.

Duration: 5–10 minutes.

Repetition: No repetition, just allow yourself to fully relax and breathe deeply throughout the duration.

Benefit: Supta Baddha Konasana promotes deep relaxation, reduces stress, and opens the hips and chest. It also improves circulation, alleviates menstrual discomfort, and enhances digestion. This pose is used for encouraging mindfulness and a sense of inner peace, making it beneficial for overall well-being and emotional balance.

3. Forward Fold (Uttanasana)

How to do this: Stand with your feet hip-width apart. Hinge at your hips and slowly fold forward, bringing your chest towards your thighs. Let your head and neck relax, and allow your arms to hang down or hold opposite elbows. If needed, slightly bend your knees to relieve tension in your hamstrings.

Repetition: 1–3 times

Duration: 2–3 minutes, taking a few deep breaths in between

Benefits: The Forward Fold (Uttanasana) stretches the hamstrings, calves, and spine, promoting flexibility. It calms the mind, reduces stress, and alleviates anxiety. The pose improves digestion, stimulates the liver and kidneys, and can help relieve headaches and insomnia. It also enhances blood circulation to the brain, promoting mental clarity and focus.

4. Puppy Pose (Uttana Shishosana)

How to do this: Start on all fours with your wrists under your shoulders and knees under your hips. Walk your hands forward, lowering your chest towards the floor while keeping your hips elevated. Rest your forehead or chin on the mat, and allow your chest to sink towards the ground. Keep your arms extended, feeling a stretch in your shoulders and upper back.

Repetition: 2–3 times, allowing a brief rest in-between.
Duration: Hold for 1–2 minutes.

Benefits: Puppy Pose deeply stretches the spine, shoulders, and chest, relieving tension and improving flexibility. It helps reduce stress and anxiety by calming the mind and promoting relaxation. This pose also eases lower back tightness, enhances overall mobility, and provides a grounding effect for stability

5. Happy Baby Pose (Ananda Balasana)

How to do this: Lie on your back and bring your knees towards your chest. Grab the outer edges of your feet with your hands, opening your knees wider than your torso. Gently pull your feet down towards your armpits, keeping your ankles aligned with your knees.

Rock gently side to side if it feels comfortable, massaging your lower back.

Repetition: 2–3 times, focusing on deep, slow breaths.

Duration: Hold for 1–3 minutes.

Benefits: Happy Baby Pose promotes flexibility and eases stress by gently stretching the inner thighs, hips, and lower back. By centering the body, it also eases mental tension and promotes relaxation.

6. Heart Opener (Supported Fish Pose)

How to do this: Place a bolster or rolled-up blanket horizontally on your mat. Sit in front of the bolster with your knees bent and feet flat on the floor. Slowly lower your back onto the bolster, allowing your head to rest comfortably. Extend your legs out straight or keep your knees bent, and open your arms out to the sides with palms facing up.

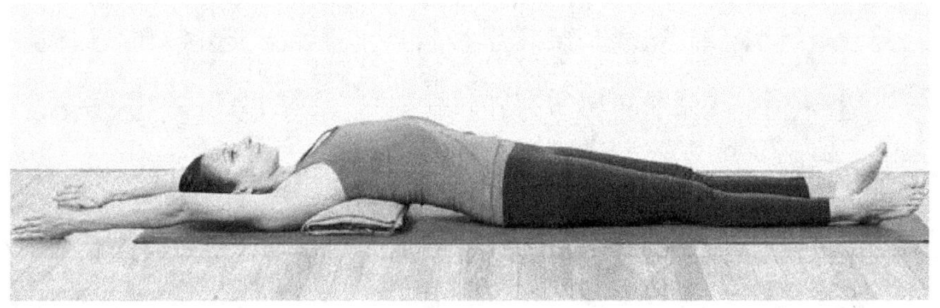

Duration: 5–10 minutes, focusing on deep, slow breaths.

Repetition: There are no repetitions, hold the pose and just relax and open your chest.

Benefits: The Heart Opener Pose widens the chest and shoulders, which improves posture and respiration. It relaxes the upper body, encourages emotional discharge, and boosts feelings of openness, positivity, and happiness. This pose also reduces stress and promotes overall well-being by encouraging deep, soothing breaths.

7. Supported Frog Pose (Salamba Mandukasana)

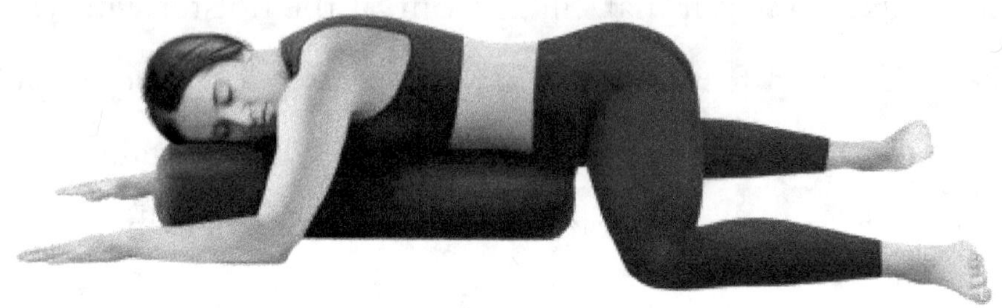

How to do this: Start on all fours with your knees wider than hip-width apart. Slowly lower your forearms to the ground, and if comfortable, place a bolster or blankets under your chest and hips for support. Allow your hips to sink down towards the floor, feeling a gentle stretch in your inner thighs and groin. Relax your head and neck, and breathe deeply.

Duration: Hold for 3–5 minutes

Repetition: Repeat 1-2 times, with a brief rest in between

Benefits: Supported Frog Pose gently opens the hips, stretches the inner thighs, and relaxes the lower back. It promotes deep relaxation, stress reduction, and attentive breathing, making it great for releasing physical and emotional strain.

The Need for Guided Imagery in Somatic Yoga for Trauma Recovery

Guided Imagery

Guided imagery is an effective therapeutic technique used in somatic yoga for trauma recovery. This technique employs the mind's eye to generate soothing and healing images that promote relaxation, reduce stress, and aid in emotional healing.

Incorporating guided imagery into your somatic yoga practices can significantly improve trauma recovery effectiveness, offering a gentle yet powerful way to heal and restore balance.

Below are some guided imageries you can practice for your trauma recovery and healing process

- **Safe Place Visualization**: To accomplish this, imagine yourself in a peaceful environment. Close your eyes and imagine a place that evokes feelings of peace and security. This could be an actual or imagined location. Engage all of your senses in the visualization. Notice the sights, sounds, smells, and textures of your peaceful environment. As you continue to visualize this for several minutes, concentrate on the sensations of calmness and security. This practice helps create a mental sanctuary for relaxation and comfort.

- **Nature Visualization**: Picture yourself in a serene natural setting, like a forest or beach. Visualize the sights, sounds, and smells, and let the peacefulness of nature soothe your mind.

Self-Massage

Self-massage in somatic yoga for trauma recovery entails applying gentle, mindful touch to relieve tension and promote relaxation. This technique allows people to connect with their bodies, reducing physical discomfort and calming the nervous system.

It promotes emotional healing by instilling a sense of safety and self-care. Self-massage can be especially effective in areas where trauma has been stored, reducing muscle tightness and improving circulation. Overall, self-massage is an effective tool for trauma recovery, increasing body awareness and facilitating a comprehensive healing process.

Where and how to apply self-massage

- **Hand and Foot Massage**: Use gentle pressure to massage your hands and feet, focusing on areas of tension to promote relaxation and enhances body awareness.

- **Facial Massage**: Gently massage your forehead, temples, and jaw to release tension and promote relaxation.

By adding these practices into your Somatic Yoga regimen, you will be able to successfully manage anxiety and panic attacks, safely process and release emotions, and utilize yoga as a powerful self-calming technique. These tactics have a way of improving your emotional control, and also help with your entire well-being and healing process.

Chapter 8: Somatic Yoga for Post-Traumatic Growth

In this chapter, we'll look into the amazing power of healing that can emerge even from the toughest traumatic experiences. We'll explore how Somatic Yoga can be a powerful tool for rebuilding your life after trauma. It's about rediscovering your strength, finding new purpose, and reconnecting with your true self. We'll also talk about the importance of self-care and kindness as you embark on this journey of healing.

Cultivating Resilience through Somatic Yoga

Resilience is the ability to bounce back from adversity, to recover and adapt in the face of challenges. For trauma survivors, building resilience is a crucial part of the healing process. Somatic Yoga offers a pathway to develop resilience by reconnecting with your body, increasing mindfulness, and promoting physical and emotional strength. Let's look at some of the ways to build resilience through Somatic Yoga

Consistent Practice

Consistent practice is essential for building resilience, as it reinforces positive habits and strengthens coping mechanisms.

- **Daily Routine:** Establishing a regular Somatic Yoga routine helps create stability and predictability in your life. Daily practice, even if just for a few minutes, reinforces resilience by providing a reliable structure and a sense of accomplishment.

- **Progressive Challenges:** Gradually increasing the complexity and intensity of your yoga practices helps build both physical and mental resilience. This might include advancing from basic poses to more challenging ones, or extending the duration of your sessions.

Mindfulness and Presence

Mindfulness and presence are essential in somatic yoga for trauma recovery and healing. By concentrating on the present moment and bodily sensations, you can reconnect with your body in a safe and nonjudgmental way. This exercise relaxes the nervous system, reduces anxiety, and releases stored trauma. Mindfulness promotes self-awareness and emotional control, helping people to better process and integrate traumatic events, resulting in holistic healing and inner peace.

- **Body Awareness Exercises:** Engaging in exercises that heighten body awareness helps you stay present and connected to your physical sensations. Practices like mindful walking or focused attention on specific body parts during yoga poses strengthen your ability to remain grounded during stressful times.

- **Meditative Practices:** Incorporating meditation into your Somatic Yoga routine cultivates mental resilience. Techniques such as mindfulness meditation or loving-kindness meditation can enhance emotional stability and improve your capacity to handle difficult emotions.

Emotional Regulation

Another important part of somatic yoga for trauma recovery and healing is Emotional control. This technique helps people control their emotions via mindful movement, breath work, and body awareness. It enables you to detect and release suppressed emotions, which reduces anxiety and improves overall emotional well-being.

- **Breath Control:** Techniques like diaphragmatic breathing or the 4-7-8 breathing method help regulate the nervous system and manage stress responses. Regular practice of these techniques enhances your ability to stay calm and centered in challenging situations.

- **Grounding Techniques:** Grounding exercises, such as standing poses or visualizing roots extending from your feet into the earth, creates a sense of stability and security, which are essential for building resilience.

Finding Meaning and Purpose in Trauma Recovery

Finding meaning and purpose in the aftermath of trauma can be transformative. It allows you to reframe your experiences and create a narrative that supports healing and growth. Somatic Yoga facilitates this process by encouraging introspection, self-discovery, and a deeper connection to your inner self.

Reflective Practices

Reflective practices in somatic yoga for trauma recovery and healing involve introspection and self-awareness. These practices, such as journaling, meditation, and mindful observation, help individuals process their experiences and emotions. By reflecting on your bodily sensations and emotional responses, you can gain insights into your trauma, identify patterns, and develop healthier coping mechanisms. Reflective practices enhance self-understanding and support the integration of healing experiences, building a deeper connection to yourself and promoting overall emotional and mental well-being.

- **Journaling:** Complement your Somatic Yoga practice with journaling to explore your thoughts and emotions. Reflecting on your experiences, progress, and insights gained through yoga can help you uncover deeper meanings and develop a sense of purpose.

- **Visualization:** Use guided visualizations during your yoga practice to imagine yourself overcoming challenges and achieving your goals. Visualizing positive outcomes and future aspirations reinforces a sense of purpose and direction.

Connecting with Inner Values

Connecting with inner values involves aligning with what truly matters to you as an individual. This practice encourages reflection on personal beliefs and goals, helping you build a sense of purpose and direction.

- **Intention Setting:** Begin each yoga session by setting an intention that aligns with your core values and aspirations. This practice helps you stay focused on what truly matters to you and infuses your practice with a sense of purpose.

- **Value-Based Actions:** Identify actions that reflect your inner values and incorporate them into your daily life. This might include acts of kindness, pursuing a passion, or engaging in activities that bring you joy and fulfillment.

Community Engagement

Engaging with a supportive community in somatic yoga for trauma recovery promotes a sense of belonging and shared healing. It provides emotional support, reduces feelings of isolation, and encourages mutual growth. By connecting with others, you can share experiences, gain insights, and build resilience, that helps enhance your overall recovery journey.

- **Yoga Classes:** Participating in group yoga classes promotes a sense of community and shared purpose. Engaging with others on a similar healing journey provides support, encouragement, and a collective sense of meaning.

- **Volunteer Work:** Use your Somatic Yoga practice as a foundation for engaging in volunteer work or community service. Helping others can create a profound sense of purpose and reinforce your resilience.

Nurturing Self-Compassion and Self-Care Practices

Self-compassion and self-care are fundamental components of trauma recovery. They involve treating yourself with kindness, understanding, and care, particularly during difficult times. Somatic Yoga promotes these qualities by encouraging a gentle, nurturing approach to your body and mind.

Self-Compassionate Mindset

Cultivating a self-compassionate mindset in somatic yoga for trauma recovery involves treating oneself with kindness and understanding. This approach helps alleviate self-criticism, promotes emotional healing, and enhances resilience. By practicing self-compassion, individuals can navigate their recovery journey with greater ease and acceptance, promoting overall well-being.

- **Loving-Kindness Meditation:** Incorporate loving-kindness meditation into your yoga practice to cultivate self-compassion. This involves silently repeating phrases of goodwill towards yourself, such as "May I be happy, may I be healthy, may I be at peace."

- **Positive Affirmations:** Use positive affirmations during your yoga practice to reinforce a compassionate self-view. Statements like "I am worthy of love and care" or "I am doing my best" can help shift your mindset towards greater self-acceptance.

Restorative Practices

Restorative practices in somatic yoga for trauma recovery focus on relaxation and stress relief. These gentle poses and mindful techniques help release tension, calm the nervous system, and promote healing. By integrating restorative practices, individuals can enhance their emotional well-being, support physical recovery, and cultivate a deep sense of inner peace.

- **Restorative Yoga:** Integrate restorative yoga poses into your routine to promote deep relaxation and self-care. Poses like Child's Pose, Supported Bridge Pose, and Legs Up the Wall are designed to release tension and soothe the nervous system.

- **Yoga Nidra:** This is also known as "yogic sleep," it is a guided meditation practice that promotes deep relaxation and healing. This practice helps you connect with a sense of inner peace and rejuvenation, building a compassionate relationship with yourself.

Holistic Self-Care

Holistic self-care in somatic yoga involves nurturing the mind, body, and spirit. It includes practices like mindful movement, breath work, meditation, and self-compassion. These techniques promote healing, reduce stress, and enhance overall well-being. By integrating holistic self-care, individuals can support their trauma recovery journey and achieve a balanced, healthy life.

- **Nourishing Activities:** Identify activities that nourish your body, mind, and spirit, and incorporate them into your self-care routine. This might include taking nature walks, enjoying a warm bath, practicing creative arts, or spending time with loved ones.

- **Boundaries and Balance:** Use your Somatic Yoga practice to develop awareness of your personal boundaries and the importance of balance in your life. Learn to recognize when you need rest, solitude, or connection, and honor those needs with compassion and care.

By integrating these practices into your Somatic Yoga routine, you can cultivate resilience, find deeper meaning and purpose in your trauma recovery, and nurture self-compassion and self-care. These elements not only support your healing journey but also empower you to live a more fulfilling and balanced life.

Part IV: Applying Somatic Yoga in Everyday Life

The part is all about bringing the calming, restorative power of Somatic Yoga into your daily routine in a way that feels natural and doable. I understand that in most cases, our daily activities may hinder us from performing these practices, which is why I have also found a way to help you incorporate it into your everyday life.

You'll learn how even the busiest among us can find simple, effective ways to manage stress through quick yoga practices like Chair Yoga and mindful breathing techniques. These aren't time-consuming rituals but brief moments of connection and relaxation that you can fit into your hectic schedule, whether at your desk, during a short break, or even while getting ready for bed.

Chapter 9: Somatic Yoga for Daily Stress Management

In this chapter, we'll look at how you can use the power of Somatic Yoga as a tool in your daily life to relax and overcome stress. You'll learn basic techniques that can turn stressful days into moments of peace, quiet, and clarity. By incorporating the Somatic yoga practices shared here, you will be able to face challenges of everyday life with greater ease, resilience, and a better sense of well-being.

Quick Somatic Yoga Practices for Busy Days

For many, finding time for a full yoga session can be challenging amidst the hustle and bustle of daily life. Fortunately, Somatic Yoga offers quick practices that can be seamlessly integrated into even the busiest schedules. These short practices can help you release tension, reset your mind, and maintain a sense of calm throughout the day.

1. Chair Yoga

• Seated Cat-Cow

How to do this: Sit upright on a chair with your feet flat on the floor. Place your hands on your knees. Inhale as you arch your back, drawing your shoulders back and lifting your chin slightly (Cow Pose). Exhale as you round your back, tucking your chin towards your chest (Cat Pose). Continue this gentle movement, synchronizing your breath with the motion. Repeat for a few breaths to release tension in your back and shoulders

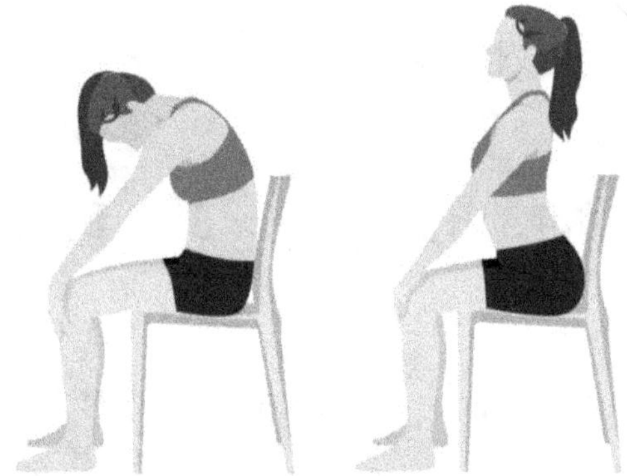

Duration: 1 –2 minutes.

Repetitions: 2–3 times.

Benefits: Seated Cat-Cow is a gentle spinal twist that helps improve flexibility, reduce back pain, and alleviate stress. It is a suitable pose for beginners and can be done anytime, anywhere.

- ## **Seated Forward Bend**

How to do this: Sit upright on the edge of a chair with your feet flat on the floor. Inhale as you lengthen your spine, reaching towards the ceiling. Exhale as you hinge forward from your hips, folding your upper body towards your legs. You can rest your hands on your legs, ankles, or feet, or if your flexibility allows, reach for your toes. This pose helps to release tension in the lower back and hamstrings.

Duration: 1–2 minutes.

Repetitions: 2–3 times.

Benefits: Seated Forward Bend helps to improve flexibility in the hamstrings and lower back, while also calming the mind. It can help relieve stress and tension.

• **Seated Eagle Arms**

How to do this: Sit upright on a chair with your feet flat on the floor. Extend your arms straight out in front of you at shoulder height. Cross your right arm over your left, bending your elbows and bringing your palms together as if you're trying to clasp your hands. If you can't touch your palms, bring them as close as possible. Lift your elbows slightly, creating a gentle stretch in your shoulders. Hold for a few breaths. Release and repeat on the other side.

Duration: Hold each side for 30 sec to 1 minute

Repetitions: 2–3 times on each side.

Benefits: Seated Eagle Arms helps to improve shoulder flexibility, strength, and range of motion. It also helps to relieve tension and stiffness in the upper back and neck.

2. Standing Poses

• Mountain Pose (Tadasana)

How to do this: Stand tall with your feet hip-width apart, and your arms relaxed by your sides. Ground yourself by pressing your feet evenly into the floor. Inhale and lift your arms overhead, palms facing each other. Lengthen your spine as you reach towards the sky. Exhale and lower your arms back to your sides.

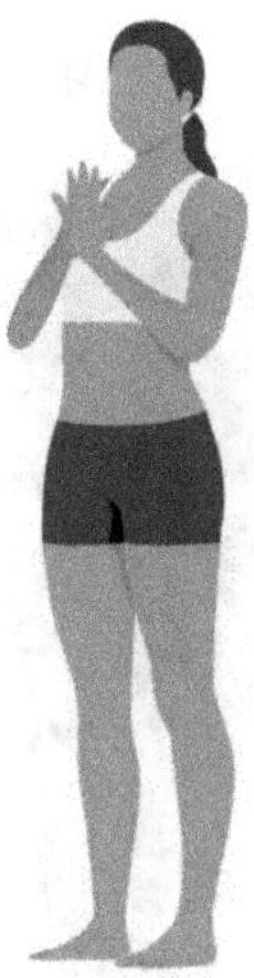

Duration: Hold the pose for a few breaths.

Repetitions: Repeat 2–3 times.

Benefits: Mountain Pose is a foundational pose that helps improve posture, balance, and body awareness. It strengthens the legs, ankles, and core while also calming the mind.

• **Standing Forward Bend (Uttanasana)**

How to do this: Stand with your feet hip-width apart, and your hands on your hips. Inhale as you lengthen your spine, reaching towards the ceiling. Exhale as you fold forward from your hips, keeping your back flat. You can bend your knees slightly to avoid straining your hamstrings. Let your hands rest on the floor, your shins, or your ankles, or if your flexibility allows, reach for your toes.

Duration: 1– 3 minutes.

Repetitions: Repeat 2–3 times.

Benefits: Standing Forward Bend is a deep stretch for the hamstrings, calves, and lower back. It helps to improve flexibility, reduce stress, and calm the mind.

3. Breathing Techniques

Alternate Nostril Breathing (Nadi Shodhana): Sit comfortably with your spine straight. Close your right nostril with your right thumb and inhale through your left nostril. Close your left nostril with your right ring finger and exhale through your right nostril. Inhale through your right nostril, then close it and exhale through your left nostril. Repeat for a few cycles to balance your energy and calm your mind.

4-7-8 Breathing: Inhale through your nose for a count of 4, hold your breath for a count of 7, and exhale through your mouth for a count of 8. Repeat for a few cycles to reduce stress and promote relaxation.

Incorporating Somatic Yoga into Daily Routines

Integrating Somatic Yoga into your daily routine doesn't require significant time commitments. Instead, it involves weaving mindful practices into the fabric of your everyday activities. By doing so, you can create a lifestyle that supports continuous well-being and stress management.

1. Morning Routine

- **Wake-Up Stretch:** Begin your day with a gentle full-body stretch while still in bed. Extend your arms overhead and stretch your legs out long, taking a deep breath. This simple practice can help you wake up your body and mind.

- **Mindful Morning Walk:** It is a good practice to start your day with a short outdoor walk. Focus on your breath and the sensations of your body as you walk. This practice can set a positive tone for the day and enhance your mindfulness.

2. Workday Breaks

- **Desk Stretching**: Take a few minutes every hour to stand up and stretch. Incorporate simple movements like shoulder rolls, neck stretches, and gentle twists to alleviate tension from sitting for prolonged periods.

- **Mindful Breathing**: Set a reminder to practice mindful breathing throughout the day. Take a few deep breaths, focusing on the sensation of the breath entering and leaving your body. This practice can help you stay grounded and reduce stress.

3. Evening Routine

- **Wind-Down Yoga**: Incorporate a short yoga session into your evening routine to help your body and mind unwind. Gentle poses like Child's Pose, Legs Up the Wall, and Reclining Bound Angle Pose can promote relaxation and prepare you for restful sleep.

- **Gratitude Practice**: Before bed, take a few moments to reflect on three things you are grateful for. This practice can shift your focus to positive aspects of your day and enhance your overall sense of well-being.

Using Somatic Yoga to Enhance Overall Well-Being

Beyond managing stress, Somatic Yoga can significantly enhance your overall well-being by promoting physical health, emotional balance, and mental clarity. By adopting a holistic approach to your practice, you can experience profound benefits in various aspects of your life.

1. Physical Health

- **Flexibility and Strength**: Regular Somatic Yoga practice helps improve flexibility and build strength. Poses that focus on stretching and strengthening muscles can enhance your physical health and reduce the risk of injuries.

- **Posture and Alignment**: Somatic Yoga emphasizes body awareness and proper alignment, which can improve your posture and reduce chronic pain associated with poor posture.

2. Emotional Balance

- **Stress Reduction**: Practices such as mindful breathing, gentle movements, and relaxation techniques can significantly reduce stress and anxiety levels. By incorporating these practices into your daily routine, you can maintain emotional balance even in challenging situations.

- **Emotional Awareness**: Somatic Yoga encourages you to tune into your body and emotions. By developing a deeper awareness of your emotional state, you can better understand and manage your feelings, leading to greater emotional resilience.

3. Mental Clarity:

- **Focus and Concentration**: Mindfulness practices in Somatic Yoga enhance your ability to focus and concentrate. Techniques such as breath awareness and meditation can sharpen your mental clarity and improve cognitive function.

- **Mind-Body Connection**: Somatic Yoga is like a gentle whisper to your body and mind, helping them reconnect and find harmony. By tuning into your physical sensations and inner thoughts, you can cultivate a deeper understanding of yourself and experience a profound sense of calm.

In this chapter, we saw how we can apply Somatic Yoga to our everyday life. Bringing these practices into your everyday life can work wonders for your mind and body. You'll feel less stressed, happier, and more balanced. Somatic Yoga is a simple yet powerful way to find peace amidst the hustle and bustle of modern life. It's a tool that can help you feel better and live life to the fullest. Hope you keep the practice going and continue to find peace and happiness as you continue.

Recap of Key Concepts in This Book

Somatic Yoga is a powerful practice that integrates the mind and body to heal trauma and promote overall well-being. Throughout this book, we have explored various aspects of Somatic Yoga and its application in trauma recovery. Let's recap the key concepts covered

Understanding Trauma

Trauma is an emotional and physical response to distressing events that overwhelm an individual's ability to cope. It can manifest in various forms, such as acute, chronic, and complex trauma.

Trauma affects the body and mind, leading to symptoms like anxiety, depression, physical pain, and emotional numbness.

Principles of Somatic Yoga

Somatic Yoga focuses on the body-mind connection, emphasizing gentle movements, breath awareness, and mindfulness to release tension and promote healing.

Unlike traditional yoga, Somatic Yoga is more introspective, encouraging practitioners to tune into their bodily sensations and emotions.

The Body-Mind Connection

Trauma is stored in the body, and the nervous system plays a crucial role in trauma responses. Dysregulation of the nervous system can lead to symptoms like hyperarousal and dissociation.

Somatic Yoga helps regulate the nervous system by promoting relaxation and grounding, thereby reducing trauma symptoms.

Somatic Yoga Practices

Basic practices include gentle movements to release tension, body scans for awareness and relaxation, and mindful breathing exercises to calm the mind and body.

Advanced practices involve progressive muscle relaxation, specific yoga poses for trauma release and grounding, and partner or group activities for connection and support.

Emotional Regulation and Post-Traumatic Growth

Somatic Yoga offers techniques to manage anxiety and panic attacks, process and release emotions safely, and use yoga as a tool for self-soothing.

It also builds resilience, helping you find meaning and purpose in trauma recovery and nurturing self-compassion and self-care practices.

Integrating Somatic Yoga into Daily Life

Quick Somatic Yoga practices for busy days, incorporating yoga into daily routines, and using yoga to enhance overall well-being.

Encouragement for Continued Practice and Self-Care

Healing from trauma is a journey that requires patience, compassion, and dedication. As you continue to practice Somatic Yoga, remember to listen to your body and honor your own pace. Consistency is key, so try to incorporate these practices into your daily routine, even if it's just for a few minutes each day.

Self-care is an essential part of this journey. Make time for activities that nourish your body, mind, and spirit. Surround yourself with supportive people, seek professional help if needed, and be kind to yourself. Remember, healing is not a linear process; there will be ups and downs, but each step forward is progress.

Somatic Yoga Sequences for Specific Trauma Symptoms

Somatic Yoga can be tailored to address specific trauma symptoms. I have highlighted the most practice you should do if you are having s particular trauma symptom.

For Insomnia

- **Legs Up the Wall (Viparita Karani)**: Lie on your back with your legs resting vertically against a wall. This pose promotes relaxation and prepares the body for sleep.

- **Reclining Bound Angle Pose (Supta Baddha Konasana)**: Lie on your back with the soles of your feet together and knees falling open. Use props to support your knees if needed. This pose calms the nervous system and encourages restful sleep.

For Hyperarousal

- **Child's Pose (Balasana)**: Kneel on the floor, sit back on your heels, and fold forward, extending your arms in front of you. This pose helps ground and calm the body.

- **Seated Forward Bend (Paschimottanasana)**: Sit with your legs extended, and fold forward from the hips, reaching for your toes. This pose soothes the nervous system and reduces hyperarousal.

For Emotional Numbness

- **Heart Opening Pose (Anahatasana)**: Start on all fours, then walk your hands forward and lower your chest towards the ground, keeping your hips over your knees. This pose opens the heart and encourages emotional release.

- **Bridge Pose (Setu Bandhasana)**: Lie on your back with your knees bent and feet flat on the floor. Lift your hips towards the ceiling, pressing into your feet and shoulders. This pose stimulates the heart and opens the chest.

For Anxiety

- **Cat-Cow Pose:** Start on all fours, alternate between arching your back (cow) and rounding it (cat). This pose helps to synchronize movement with breath, reducing anxiety and promoting mental clarity.

- **Standing Forward Bend (Uttanasana):** Stand with your feet hip-width apart, then bend forward at the hips, letting your head and arms hang. This pose releases tension and anxiety, and also calm the mind.

For Anger

- **Warrior II (Virabhadrasana II):** Stand with your legs wide apart, turn one foot out, and bend your front knee. Extend your arms parallel to the ground. This pose helps release pent-up energy and transforms anger into focused strength.

- **Lion's Breath (Simhasana):** Kneel and sit back on your heels, then lean forward slightly, placing your hands on your knees. Open your mouth wide, stick out your tongue, and exhale forcefully with a roaring sound. This practice helps release anger and frustration.

For Dissociation:

- **Mountain Pose (Tadasana):** Stand tall with your feet together, grounding through all four corners of your feet. This pose helps to reconnect with the body and the present moment, reducing dissociation.

- **Tree Pose (Vrksasana):** Stand on one leg and place the sole of your other foot against your inner thigh or calf. This balancing pose enhances body awareness and helps bring focus back to the present.

For Depression

- **Cobra Pose (Bhujangasana):** Lie face down with your hands under your shoulders, then lift your chest while keeping your pelvis on the ground. This backbend stimulates energy flow and combats feelings of depression.

- **Legs Up the Wall (Viparita Karani):** Lie on your back with your legs resting vertically against a wall. This pose promotes circulation and helps alleviate symptoms of depression.

For Intrusive Thoughts

- **Garland Pose (Malasana):** Squat with your feet close together, bringing your hands together at your chest. This grounding pose helps clear the mind and reduces the intensity of intrusive thoughts.

- **Alternate Nostril Breathing (Nadi Shodhana):** Sit comfortably and use your thumb and ring finger to alternately close each nostril while breathing through the other. This pranayama technique balances the mind and reduces intrusive thoughts.

Tips for Practicing Somatic Yoga with Specific Trauma Populations

Different trauma populations may have unique needs when practicing Somatic Yoga. Here are some tips for working with specific groups

Veterans

- Create a safe and supportive environment, emphasizing trust and non-judgment.

- Incorporate grounding techniques to help veterans feel present and connected.

- Use gentle movements and avoid triggering poses or language.

Survivors of Abuse

- Focus on empowerment and control, allowing survivors to choose their level of participation.

- Emphasize self-compassion and body awareness, helping survivors reconnect with their bodies.

- Offer modifications and support for individuals who may have physical limitations or emotional sensitivities.

Children and Adolescents:

- Use playful and engaging activities to make Somatic Yoga enjoyable for younger kids.

- Encourage self-expression and creativity through movement and breath.

- Provide a safe and nurturing space where children and adolescents feel heard and valued.

Glossary of Somatic Yoga Terms

To support your understanding and practice of Somatic Yoga, here is a glossary of common terms used throughout this book.

1. **Somatic**: Relating to the body, especially as distinct from the mind.

2. **Grounding**: Techniques used to connect with the present moment and the physical body.

3. **Hyperarousal**: A state of increased physiological and emotional tension often experienced after trauma.

4. **Mindfulness**: The practice of being fully present and aware of the current moment without judgment.

5. **Nervous System Regulation**: Techniques used to balance the autonomic nervous system, promoting a state of calm and relaxation.

6. **Trauma Release**: The process of releasing stored trauma from the body through movement, breath, and other therapeutic practices.

7. **Body Scan**: A mindfulness practice that involves paying attention to sensations in different parts of the body.

8. **Progressive Muscle Relaxation**: A technique that involves tensing and then slowly releasing different

muscle groups to reduce tension and promote relaxation.

9. **Body-Mind Connection:** The interplay between physical and mental states, emphasizing how emotions and experiences can be stored in the body and how physical practices can influence mental well-being.

10. **Somatic Awareness:** The ability to perceive and feel bodily sensations, often used to connect with internal experiences and emotions.

11. **Vagus Nerve:** A key component of the parasympathetic nervous system that helps regulate stress responses, promote relaxation, and maintain a balanced state of being.

12. **Trauma-Informed Practice:** An approach that recognizes the impact of trauma on individuals and integrates this understanding into the practice to create a safe and supportive environment.

13. **Emotional Regulation:** Techniques and practices aimed at managing and balancing emotional responses, particularly in the context of trauma recovery.

14. **Autonomic Nervous System (ANS):** The part of the nervous system responsible for controlling involuntary bodily functions, such as heart rate, digestion, and

respiration, and its regulation is critical in trauma recovery.

15. **Hypervigilance:** An enhanced state of sensory sensitivity and an exaggerated state of awareness, often resulting from trauma.

16. **Trauma-Informed Yoga:** A specialized form of yoga that is adapted to be sensitive to the needs of individuals who have experienced trauma, focusing on safety, empowerment, and choice.

17. **Restorative Yoga:** A gentle form of yoga that emphasizes relaxation and the use of props to support the body, facilitating deep rest and recovery.

18. **Neuroplasticity:** The brain's ability to reorganize itself by forming new neural connections, which can be influenced by practices like Somatic Yoga to support healing and recovery.

19. **Embodiment:** The experience of being fully present in one's body, often cultivated through somatic practices to enhance self-awareness and healing.

20. **Dissociation:** A mental process of disconnecting from one's thoughts, feelings, memories, or sense of identity, which can occur as a response to trauma.

21. **Interoception:** The sense of the internal state of the

body, including awareness of bodily sensations like hunger, thirst, and emotional responses.

22. **Grounded Breathing:** A specific breathing technique used to anchor oneself in the present moment, promoting a sense of stability and calm.

23. **Adaptive Response:** The body's natural mechanisms for coping with stress or trauma, which can be supported and strengthened through somatic practices.

24. **Polyvagal Theory:** A theory that explains how the vagus nerve influences emotional regulation, social connection, and our response to trauma.

25. **Safe Space:** A physical or mental environment where one feels secure, supported, and free from harm or judgment, crucial for effective trauma recovery practices.